THE MONOPOLY TOUR OF LONDON

BY
HENRY HOXTON

To make suggestions or comments on how to improve future editions of this book, or for any other reason, you can contact the author by email at: henryhoxton@mail.com

CONTENTS

INTRODUCTION — Page 1

TRAVEL COSTS IN LONDON — Page 5

THE BROWN GROUP
OLD KENT ROAD — Page 10
WHITECHAPEL ROAD — Page 14

KING'S CROSS STATION AND THE LIGHT BLUE GROUP
KINGS CROSS STATION — Page 20
THE ANGEL ISLINGTON — Page 22
EUSTON ROAD — Page 24
PENTONVILLE ROAD — Page 26

THE PINK GROUP
PALL MALL — Page 30
WHITEHALL — Page 34
NORTHUMBERLAND AVENUE — Page 38

MARYLEBONE STATION AND THE ORANGE GROUP
MARYLEBONE STATION — Page 42
BOW STREET — Page 44
MARLBOROUGH STREET — Page 48
VINE STREET — Page 52

THE RED GROUP
STRAND — Page 56
FLEET STREET — Page 60
TRAFALGAR SQUARE — Page 64

FENCHURCH STREET STATION AND THE YELLOW GROUP
FENCHURCH STREET STATION — Page 68
LEICESTER SQUARE — Page 70
COVENTRY STREET — Page 74
PICCADILLY — Page 76

THE GREEN GROUP
REGENT STREET — Page 82
OXFORD STREET — Page 84
BOND STREET — Page 86

LIVERPOOL STREET STATION — Page 90

THE DARK BLUE GROUP
PARK LANE — Page 98
MAYFAIR — Page 102

ALTERNATIVES — Page 105

Introduction

Most visitors to a city naturally want to see the usual famous tourist sights, but there is much more to see as well and for those who like to do something a bit different, see some of the less usual sights and explore London without being overly adventurous or going too far off the beaten track, I have created this guided tour of London based on the famous board game, Monopoly. There are twenty-six named properties on the Monopoly board, including the four stations and this guide will take you to all of them.

The Electric Company and the Waterworks are too ambiguous to fit into this tour, however, for those who want to include them, you could view Battersea Power Station, which is now a shopping mall and if you want a special experience, take the elevator in the north-west chimney for a 360-degree view of London. For the Waterworks, Crossness Pumping Station in Bexley, south-east London is a marvel of Victorian engineering and has been described as a Cathedral of Ironwork. It is a delight for students of architecture.

It's logical to start at "GO" and stop at each of the properties in sequence, therefore this tour visits each of the properties in the order that they appear on the Monopoly board, however, it is impossible not to interrupt that order by venturing into one or more properties out of sequence, as you will discover later, but I have kept to the correct order as closely as is possible.

Here are four suggested ways in which to take the tour;
(1) By visiting each property in the order it appears in the game and in this guide, which may be the shortest way around the board but it is certainly not the shortest way around the city. Everybody walks at different speeds and will take differing amounts of time for sightseeing, so it's impossible to accurately gauge how long it will take to complete this tour if you stick to the board sequence, however, I think you should probably allow yourself four or five days to do it all, especially if you're an ambler, like me.

You can split the tour into different colour groups and visit each of those groups in days or half-days, according to how you feel.

(2) If you're not bothered about which order you visit each property, then you can, of course, avoid doubling back on your travelling by putting a bit of thought into planning your route. The two properties in the brown group, for example, are quite a distance from each other and on opposite sides of the river, as well as being the most southerly and most eastern properties on the board. Strand is at one end of the red group, whereas in reality it is between the other two properties. Liverpool Street station pops up between two west end groups and requires a trip across the city and back again if you stick to the board sequence, but it is easy to visit with a ten-minute walk from Fenchurch Street station while you are close to that. Therefore Monopoly geeks who just want to visit all the properties in any sequence will probably prefer to visit them in a more geographically time-efficient order, which can be done comfortably in half a day and they get to tick all the boxes, although that is dependent on doing the tour without spending much time sightseeing.

You can use the Tube or buses, of course, but you can also walk the roughly 20 kilometres route in around five or six hours. Or if you're fit enough and brave enough to tackle the London traffic, you might consider using one of the Santander cycles that you will see dotted around London. You can buy an access card at the cycle docking station and return the cycle to a different docking station, so you don't have to bring it back to the one where you picked it up. I believe you can "do" all the Monopoly properties on a bicycle in around an hour and a half, possibly a bit quicker on a Sunday morning, when there is less traffic. There are lots of cyclists in London, but it wouldn't be my preferred method of travel in the city, or in any city for that matter.

(3) The third way is arguably how most visitors will get the best use from this guide; you can read each of the walks as described in this

book, then select one or more colour groups (as suggested in (1)) that interest you the most and visit those groups in any order that suits your time and plans for your vacation. You may, for instance, decide that Old Kent Road is not a priority for you, but you may want to spend more time doing the walk around the Liverpool Street station area. If this your preferred way to explore London then I suggest doing a little additional research and prioritising the "mini-tours" of Liverpool Street Station, the Pink Group and the Red Group and try to add the Orange Group and Light Blue Group if you have time. The Green Group and Dark Blue Group are, in my opinion, the least interesting walks.

(4) The fourth way is undoubtedly the longest, although it does introduce an element of surprise to the tour. You can throw a couple of dice, just as you would in the game, then visit the property that you would land on.

This book also provides a short dialogue on each property along with a little history, some local information and a few suggestions for other things worth seeing nearby. I would recommend that you do a little research of your own and include other nearby places to each property, because there is far too much for me to include in this guide and it is therefore necessarily brief. However, whether you do extra research or not, you will be pleasantly surprised at how many of London's usual tourist attractions can be viewed or visited whilst enjoying this tour, many of them for free.

There are a couple of odd points worth noting on the London Monopoly board. Purists may be disappointed to learn that it is impossible to visit all the properties in the specific order they appear on the board without venturing into adjacent properties at some point, although I have tried to keep the tour as free from 'trespass' as I can. There are also a few properties which don't actually exist as physical entities but are areas, or concepts, rather than specific places. These will be explained and will become clear later, as we reach them during the tour.

A good street map is invaluable, of course, so either buy an A to Z map book of London or download one to your phone, although Google Maps or Apple Maps usually work fine too.

London is not blessed with a wealth of public toilets, but most big stores, restaurants and pubs have them, although the restaurants and pubs will usually expect you to buy something, telling you that the toilet is for customers' use only, so it's good advice to combine your refreshment breaks with visits to the toilet, even if you don't have a pressing need at the time, because you may not find another one quickly when you want it.

Although we will use the London Underground, or Tube, for the longer stretches of this tour, do remember that as with most tours, there is a fair bit of walking involved as well, so make sure you have suitable shoes for walking and appropriate clothing for the prevailing weather.

There are plenty of shops along the way where you can buy drinks and snacks, so don't waste your energy by carrying too many with you, although a bottle of water is always useful, especially in the hot summer. You will also find lots of restaurants, cafes, snack bars and pubs to have lunch, most are reasonably priced but there are some not-so-reasonably priced ones too, so be sure to check the prices before ordering, especially in the West End.

There are some blank pages and blank spaces throughout this book, where you can make notes to refresh your memory when you later look back at the photographs you have taken. I hope this will help you to create a lasting and special memory of your visit to London.

For ease of carrying, this book is a handy size and has a soft cover, however, for those who want to create a more substantial memory, there is also a hardcover version available from Amazon.

Travel costs in London
The best way to explore London is by walking and by using public transport to cover longer distances. There are several ways to pay for your travel on public transport, including buying a travelcard or a visitors Oyster card, but the most convenient way is to use your contactless debit or credit card to tap in and out of the service. You can also use your smartphone or Apple Watch if that's your preferred payment method. Your contactless card will work the same way as a travelcard. The system will charge your card at the end of the day and will calculate the best price for you, so if your total travel cost comes to less than the cost of a travelcard, you will be charged for the lower cost, but if your total number of journeys exceeds the price of a travelcard the cost is capped and you will only be charged the price of a travelcard.

There are a few things to be aware of, though;
You can only use one card for each person travelling, so if you are a couple you will need two cards, although two cards linked to a joint bank account is usually ok as the system charges each card individually.
Always use the same card to tap in and out; if you use two different cards the system may not work, or worse, you might be charged twice.
The contactless system will charge an adult fare, so don't use it for children, instead, you can buy a child-rate travelcard for children. Check your needs before buying a child rate card, because one child under five travel can travel free with each fare-paying adult. Also, if your child is under 11, they can travel free on Buses and trams, the Tube, DLR, London Overground, Elizabeth Line and some National Rail services.
At the time of writing, (early 2023), an adult one-day travelcard for all zones costs £21.50. There is a cheaper one costing £15.20. which is restricted to use outside of peak travel times and might be of interest at weekends, but the rush-hour time restrictions from Monday to Friday probably won't suit most people who want to use their time effectively.

Enquire about zonal travelcards, which restrict you to just zones 1 and 2, but those are probably the zones you really need and the daily cap is only £8.10.

If your group is ten or more people then ask at a station about a group travelcard, which has further discounts.

Finally, check that the system recognises your card, as it is designed for UK cards and if your card was issued in another country it may not work, in which case I would suggest enquiring at any Tube station about using travelcards or buying a visitor's Oyster card, which is essentially a pre-paid contactless card for use on London's transport network.

So, having got yourself prepared, let's get on with the tour. You will need to start by getting from wherever you are to Elephant and Castle Tube station.

The Brown Group

Photograph of Old Kent Road at the intersection of Dunton Road near "The Dun Cow". Photographed by en:user:SoxFan April 2005 and shared under licence CC BY-SA 3.0

Getting to Old Kent Road

Start your tour by going to Elephant and Castle Tube station. Elephant and Castle station is on the Northern Line and the Bakerloo Line.

Old Kent Road is the only Monopoly property south of the River Thames and it is also the most remote property from a Tube station, so there is about a half-hour walk to get to it, but it is fairly flat and much of the walk is through some of South London's pleasant open spaces.

Leave the station via the Newington Butts exit, turn left and head south along Newington Butts then turn left into Walworth Road.

Turn into Elephant Park and enjoy a stroll through one of south London's many leafy spaces.

Leave the park at the far end and turn right into Ash Avenue, then at the end of Ash Avenue turn left into Rodney Place. Opposite, you will see another park, the Victory Community Park. Walk straight through Victory Community Park and come out onto Balfour Street. Turn right and walk along Balfour Street until you reach Chatham Street, then turn left into Chatham Street and continue walking past Salisbury Row Park and the play area.

At the end of Chatham Street, bear left and continue along Darwin Street until you reach the main A201 road, then turn right. Walk past Mason Street and continue until you are almost at Preston Close, then cross the main road.

You have just crossed Old Kent Road.

Nearby Attractions

The Imperial War Museum is close to Elephant and Castle Tube station and has free entry, although there may be a charge for special events. If you want to visit the IWM you should do so before heading to Old Kent Road, as you won't be returning to Elephant and Castle. After Old Kent Road we will continue to Tower Bridge and the Tower of London.

Old Kent Road itself was originally a Roman road and was the main artery between London and Kent, which it still is today and consequently it is almost always chock-a-block with busy traffic. It is built up with high-rise apartment blocks, large shops and even larger trading depots, making it a not particularly pleasant road to visit, but as it is the first property on the Monopoly board, it is the place where we must start our tour.

However, the walking route from here on hopefully makes up for the disappointing Old Kent Road itself.

Once you arrive at Old Kent Road it's really not worth the walk back to Elephant and Castle, (for reference, the Tube from Elephant and Castle to Whitechapel takes around 30 minutes anyway), so my recommendation is to walk to Tower Bridge, which takes about fifteen minutes.

Go back to the large traffic roundabout at Ring Road Square, then turn right onto Tower Bridge Road. Walk up to Abbey Street, then cross the road to look at St Mary Magdalen Churchyard, where there has been a church on the site since at least as early as 1290. Continue along Tower Bridge Road until you come to Tower Bridge and continue walking north, over Tower Bridge and across the River Thames, pausing to look at HMS Belfast, moored in the river, take in the magnificent view of the Tower of London and see London Bridge on the way.

Leaving Tower Bridge you will walk past the east side of the Tower of London, then you can turn left and see some of the 2,000-year-old remains of the Roman Wall that once surrounded the City of London.

Whitechapel Road, looking east Whitechapel station is seen on the north side of the road and is fronted by the street-market stalls. Photograph by Dr Neil Clifton. Shared under licence CC BY-SA 2.0

Getting to Whitechapel Road

Once across Tower Bridge you have a choice, to take the Tube from Tower Hill station, or to continue walking to our next destination. The Tube to Aldgate East station takes four minutes, plus waiting time, and the walk takes ten minutes. The Tube to Whitechapel station is around six minutes and walking takes around 20 minutes, but as there is more to see on foot, I would recommend continuing the walk.

Continue past the Tower of London into Tower Hill and walk past the grassy space called Tower Bridge Piazza on your left. Cross Shorter Street and stroll up Minories, taking a few minutes to look at Ibex House, a "modernistic" style office block that was built between 1933 and 1937. It is not only modernistic in its design but also in its outlook, being one of the first mixed-use buildings, incorporating a few shops and a pub (The Peacock) into the ground floor. Continue along Minories to Aldgate High Street then turn right and walk to Aldgate East station, where the road becomes Whitechapel High Street. A few minutes further on and you will see the Altab Ali Park, which is a memorial themed parked in remembrance of Altab Ali, a Bangladeshi man who was brutally murdered in a racist attack in 1978. Before being renamed, the park was known as St Mary's Park and was once the site of the small, white-painted church of St Mary Matfelon, from which the Whitechapel area takes its name.

You are now on Whitechapel Road.

Nearby attractions

Whitechapel Road was a Roman road connecting London with Colchester, which was the first Roman capital of Britain. It was and still is a busy thoroughfare, although back in the mid-19th century most of the traffic was sheep and cattle being driven to market. These days, of course, it is motor vehicles.

Whitechapel Art Gallery is close to Aldgate East and the main gallery is free to enter.

This is Jack the Ripper territory and there are several tours based on his murders, some free.

The Classic Football Shirts store is on Commercial Street, just a minute or so walk from Aldgate East station and has hundreds, if not thousands, of football shirts from around the world.

Whitechapel Road Market is based around Whitechapel station and is a lively market open Mondays to Saturdays.

If you continue walking for another five minutes or so you will come to the Royal London Hospital, which has an interesting little museum full of medical curiosities, including the skeleton of Joseph Merrick, "The Elephant Man". The museum is housed in the crypt of a 19th-century church and is free.

Across the road from the Royal London Hospital is Whitechapel Station, where you will find connections to the District and the Hammersmith & City Tube lines, as well as the Elizabeth Line and the London Overground.

Kings Cross Station and the Light Blue Group

Kings Cross, Photograph by Bert Seghers. Shared under Licence CC0

Getting to Kings Cross Station

When you're ready to continue the tour, the most direct way to get to our next destination is to catch a Hammersmith & City Tube train from Whitechapel station to Kings Cross St Pancras Tube station.

Nearby Attractions

Kings Cross St Pancras Tube station is so named because the two mainline stations sit next to each other and it's worth looking at both from the outside, but to my mind, St Pancras is by far the more attractive building and well worth the few minutes or so walk to see it. Do go inside, too, as it is arguably one of the most architecturally impressive railway stations in the world. Try not to walk as far as the road, which is Euston Road, because we will return to it later, in sequence.

According to legend, King's Cross is the site of Queen Boudica's final battle with the Romans and some people claim that she is actually buried beneath one of the platforms. Her ghost is said to haunt the station, around platforms 8–10. (I wonder if she ever bumps into Harry Potter at platform 9 ¾ ?)

Kings Cross station was built in 1851/52 by the Great Northern Railway and takes its name from a monument to King George lV which used to stand in the proximity but was demolished in 1845.

The London Canal Museum in nearby New Wharf Road is interesting if you like waterways and costs £6 per adult entry, although there is a family ticket available for £14 (2023 price) if you do want to go.

The British Museum is only a five-minute walk away and entry is free.

If you have children they will surely want to find platform 9 ¾ at Kings Cross, where there is also a Harry Potter shop for souvenirs.

There are three other Monopoly properties close to Kings Cross Station, The Angel Islington, Euston Road and Pentonville Road and although both Euston Road and Pentonville Road are closer, the next property in the order of play is The Angel Islington.

The Angel Hotel (now offices). Photo by Des Blenkinsopp. Shared under licence CC BY-SA 2.0

Getting to The Angel Islington

To get to The Angel Islington in the correct board order you should head back down to the Tube and take the Northern Line one stop to Angel.

Nearby Attractions

The Angel Islington takes its name from a hotel which doesn't exist anymore but gave its name to the surrounding area. The site of the former hotel is at the junction of Islington High Street and Pentonville Road where a coaching inn first appeared around 1225. 'The Angel', as it became known, was rebuilt in the 17th century and rebuilt again in the 19th century. During the 1960s the building became almost derelict but was refurbished as a bank during the 1980s. However, there is now a newer pub called 'The Angel' next door and we will use this as our property to visit.

Turn left out of Angel Station and cross the road, then walk down to the Angel pub, but don't go any further, or you will risk visiting the properties in an incorrect order. Once you've been to the Angel pub, cross back over the road and continue on to the junction, where you should turn left onto the major road, the A501, Goswell Road. Cross Torrens Street and shortly afterwards, cross Goswell Road onto the pedestrian traffic island, where you will see the Angel Clock, painted green and gold. The clock used to stand outside the Angel Hotel but was moved and has been in its present location since 1906 and is operated by a watch mechanism which used to be wound up by hand every day until an electric winding system was installed shortly after the relocation. It still bears the original advertisement for the maker, J. Smith & Sons, established in 1780.

Next, retrace your steps back to Upper Street, turn right and cross the road just past Angel Station, then continue walking to Camden Passage, where you can explore the outdoor market and search for treasures among the antiques, bric-a-brac and collectables always on sale there. You might also pick up a bargain piece of vintage clothing, although there are plenty of more contemporary traders, too.

Euston Road in 2008. Photograph by Stacey Harris, shared under licence CC BY-SA 2.0

Getting to Euston Road

This is another of those awkward situations where two properties in correct board order are separated by a third "property, so to maintain the correct order, when you've done your shopping you should go back to Angel station and catch the Tube for a seven-minute ride to Euston, also on the Northern Line.

Leave Euston Tube station via Euston Main Line station. In front of the main station you will see Euston Square Gardens and the bus park. There you can see the Euston memorial, which was erected by railway staff to honour their fallen comrades of both World Wars. Turn left and walk through Euston Square Gardens to Eversholt Street, then turn right. The main road at the end is Euston Road.

Nearby Attractions

Turn left onto Euston Road and walk a few minutes until you come to Midland Road, then turn left again and you will find the entrance to the British Library, which houses over 14,000,000 books on 400 miles of bookshelves and contains works as diverse as two original copies of the Magna Carta, Britain's first constitutional law book, and some hand-written songs by the Beatles.

The Lighthouse in Pentonville Road.
Photo by Oxyman shared under licence CC BY-SA 2.0

Getting to Pentonville Road

Leave the British Library back onto Euston Road and turn left. After about 15 minutes of walking and passing King's Cross station again, you will come to Joseph Grimaldi Park on your left. This is where Euston Road becomes Pentonville Road.

Nearby Attractions

Joseph Grimaldi Park is an open space constructed on the former burial ground of St James's Anglican Chapel and is named to commemorate the famous pantomime clown, Joseph Grimaldi, who is buried there.

It is a great place to let the children loose for a while, enjoy the play equipment and stretch their legs, while you rest yours.

If you go into the park via the entrance near Rodney Street you will find Joseph Grimaldi's grave.

There is also a bronze public artwork, which is shaped like two coffins and is designed to be walked on. The tiles respond to foot pressure and play musical notes. It's possible, apparently, to play a famous Grimaldi tune, "Hot Codlins", by walking on the tiles, but I think you probably have to know how the tune goes first.

When the children (or you) are rested, it will be time to head toward our next destination, which is Pall Mall.

The Pink Group

Pall Mall. Photo by Panhard, shared under Licence CC BY 2.5

Getting to Pall Mall

Walk the five minutes back to King's Cross Tube station and catch the Piccadilly Line to Piccadilly station. Upon leaving Piccadilly station, do not cross to the Shaftesbury Memorial, we'll get back to that later. Instead, turn left then turn right into Haymarket, famous for its theatres. Walk down to Her Majesty's Theatre and turn right into Charles 2nd Street. When you reach Waterloo Place, turn left and you will come to the Crimean War Memorial and there is also a statue of Florence Nightingale. Continue to the road at the bottom and you will arrive at Pall Mall.

Nearby Attractions

Pall Mall takes its name from a game played in the 17th century, using long-handled mallets to strike balls. The game is no longer played there, but the name remains.

In 1807 Pall Mall became the first London street to be lit by gas and some of the lamp posts are almost original, dating back to 1820.

Trafalgar Square is close by, but don't go there as we'll get to that later because it's another property on the Monopoly board. Also close by are St James's Palace, St James's Park and Buckingham Palace. Instead, turn left and cross Pall Mall, walk a few minutes to the end and turn into Marlborough Road to discover St James's Palace, a 16th-century Royal Palace built by Henry Vlll. The palace is still in use and apart from its official functions it is home to Princess Anne, Princess Beatrice and Princess Alexandra. The Palace is open to the public and is well worth exploring, as are some of the surrounding historic buildings.

If you continue to the end of Marlborough Road you will come to The Mall. Turn right into The Mall and you will see the Queen Victoria Monument standing in front of Buckingham Palace.

Turn left at the roundabout of the Queen Victoria Memorial, then left again into Spur Road and left once more into Birdcage Walk.

You can go along Birdcage Walk or you can enter St James's Park here and take the scenic route, or you can enter the park by St James's Drinking Fountain, further along Birdcage Walk, but either way, you should then walk to the bridge and cross the lake. After crossing the lake, turn right and follow the lake as closely as possible until you come to the cafe, where you can enjoy a drink (and use the toilets if you need to). After the cafe, head north, back toward The Mall and you will see the South African Royal Artillery Memorial, at the junction of The Mall and Horseguards Road.

Whitehall, Showing the women of WW2 monument and the Cenotaph. Photo by Tbmurray, shared under licence CC BY 3.0

Getting to Whitehall

Our next property is an easy walk that will take less than ten minutes if you don't get too distracted on the way. At the South African Royal Artillery Memorial, walk down Horse Guards Road. Take a small diversion and turn left opposite the Guards Memorial to walk along Horse Guards Parade and back again. The back of the Household Cavalry Museum is at the end of Horse Guards Parade. When you get back to Horse Guards Road, turn left and continue past the statue of Earl Mountbatten, past the less well-known end of Downing Street and past the Churchill War Rooms, an underground suite of offices where Prime Minister Winston Churchill lived and worked during World War 2. Continue walking until you reach Great George Street, then turn left. After a minute or so you will reach Parliament Square with the garden at its centre. Turn right into Parliament Square, keeping the garden on your left and then turn right into Broad Sanctuary, where you will find Westminster Abbey on your left. Take your photos then turn around and walk back to Parliament Square, keeping the garden on your left and St Margaret's Church on your right. You will emerge into Abingdon Street, where you will see the back of Westminster Abbey on your right and Westminster Palace, the home of the British Parliament, on your left. Turn around and backtrack along Abingdon Street and turn right into Bridge Street, towards Westminster Bridge and the River Thames. Big Ben is on your right. Big Ben is actually the name of the largest bell in the peal and the structure that houses the bells and the clock is correctly called the Elizabeth Tower, but everyone calls it Big Ben.

Now cross the road and turn left, walk past Westminster Tube station and at the end of Bridge Street you will find Parliament Street on your right. Walk up Parliament Street as far as the Cenotaph, Britain's National War Memorial and remembrance site, and the road becomes Whitehall.

Nearby Attractions

Walk past the Cenotaph and see the more famous end of Downing Street, where Britain's Prime Minister has their official residence at number ten. You can't go into Downing Street, but you can peer through the iron security gates. A little further on is the monument to the Women of World War 2 and a bit further still is Banqueting House on your right and the front of the Household Cavalry Museum on your left. You don't want to go too far north, as you will get to Trafalgar Square out of board order, so turn right into Horse Guards Avenue and walk down to the river. To your right is the Royal Air Force memorial and on the other side of the river you will see the London Eye, a giant ferris wheel. Turn left out of Horse Guards Avenue and walk along the Embankment.

Northumberland Avenue from the north.
Photo by R Sones, shared under licence CC BY-SA2.0

Getting to Northumberland Avenue

Walk along Victoria Embankment for five minutes, with the River Thames on your right. Just before the Hungerford Railway Bridge, turn left into Northumberland Avenue.

Nearby Attractions

There's not much to see in the area that we haven't already covered or will cover shortly, but there is a classic Cabman's Shelter that's worth a look. These green-painted, wooden shelters were introduced to London in 1875 to provide places other than pubs, where cab drivers could get a meal and refreshments, (but alcohol was strictly forbidden).

Marylebone Station and the Orange Group

Marylebone Station.
Photo by N Chadwick, shared under licence CC SA-BY 2.0

Getting to Marylebone Station

Walk up Northumberland Avenue, past the Cabman's Shelter on your right, then turn right into Embankment Place. Walk under the bridge and as the road bends left into Villiers Street, on your right you will see an entrance to Embankment Tube Station. From Embankment you can catch a Bakerloo Line Tube train to Marylebone Station, which takes around ten minutes.

Nearby Attractions

Marylebone Station is the smallest of London's main termini and the only one which still runs diesel trains, as none of the rail lines is electrified. Because of its relative quietness, Marylebone station is often used for film-making and some of the scenes from the Beatles' film A Hard Day's Night were filmed here, as were some from Michael Caine's film, The Ipcress File.

Church Street market is a few minutes walk away and you will find a lively and friendly atmosphere in the market, as well as some cheap bargains. Lords Cricket ground is a ten-minute walk, but there's not much to see unless there's a test match going on.

You can leave Marylebone Station, turn left into Melcombe Place, then cross Melcombe Place and walk down Great Central Street to Marylebone Road. Turn left on Marylebone Road and walk along until you get to Baker Street. If you want to visit Madame Tussauds Waxwork Museum you can cross Baker Street and continue for another minute walking. Alternatively, you can turn left into Baker Street and find the Sherlock Holmes Museum, which is a popular visitor attraction, although at £16 entry for a fifteen-minute tour, it's not good value in my opinion. Take note that Baker Street Tube station is on your right, almost opposite the Sherlock Holmes Museum. If you continue up Baker Street for a few minutes and bear right where it merges with Park Road, you will come to Regent's Park, with the Serpentine and London Zoo. Entry to the park is free but you'll have to pay £28.50 to go into the Zoo.

Bow Street Magistrates Court in the 19th Century

Getting to Bow Street

Walk back to Baker Street station and take the Bakerloo Line Tube to Piccadilly Circus then change onto the Piccadilly Line to Covent Garden. Leave Covent Garden station onto James Street and turn right, then take the first turning left onto Floral Street. After two minutes you will arrive at Bow Street.

Nearby Attractions

Number 4 Bow Street was the site of the magistrates' court where the novelist, Sir Henry Fielding, created London's first recognised police force, whom he called 'thief-takers' but they became better known as the Bow Street Runners.

There is much to see and do in the Covent Garden area and it's well worth spending an hour or more just walking around and soaking up the general atmosphere, however, if you're a purist and want to visit all the properties in the correct board order, be careful not to wander too far south or you'll end up in Strand, a property which we will get to later on.

When you arrive at Bow Street, turn right to see the Royal Opera House and the Police Museum opposite it. The Police Museum is at number 28 Bow Street and costs £6 to visit, although there are sometimes discounts available for groups and concessions. You could stretch a point here and tick off "go to jail" as well and as you pay to enter but not to leave, "get out of jail free" is also possible.

Continue along Bow Street, across Russell Street until you reach Tavistock Street, then turn right and you will come to the London Transport Museum, which is well worth a visit if it's in your budget to buy an annual pass at £21 per adult, although children under 17 can go in free.

Close to the London Transport Museum is Jubilee Market, where you'll find stalls selling antiques and bric-a-brac as well as craft items. Also close is the Piazza, which is probably the main attraction for visitors, with street musicians and entertainers as well as covered areas with shops and cafes.

One of my favourite visits in the area is to **Seven Dials Market**, which is packed with food shops and eateries and where I usually choose to eat lunch, but you'll pass by there on your next walk. Also nearby is the Royal Opera House.

Liberty's Department Store on Gt Marlborough St.
Photo by John Winfield, shared under licence CC BY-SA 2.0

Getting to Marlborough Street

Marlborough Street doesn't exist. It is a shortened name for Great Marlborough Street and is named after Marlborough Street Magistrates Court. To get there from Bow Street you can either take the Piccadilly Line Tube from Covent Garden to Piccadilly, with a short walk at each end, which takes around fifteen minutes in total, or you can walk the one mile in around fifteen to twenty minutes. I recommend the walk, as it's only a few minutes longer than the Tube and of course is much more interesting.

To walk from Bow Street, turn back towards Floral Street, go past Floral Street and continue across Long Acre into Endell Street, then walk up to Shelton Street and turn left. Walk down Shelton Street to the Crown & Anchor, then turn right into Neal Street. At the end of Neal Street, turn left into Earlham Street. Walk down Earlham Street until you come to Seven Dials - a road junction with seven roads. You could take time to visit the famous market here if it's open when you visit. Continue across the junction into the other part of Earlham Street and walk to Shaftesbury Avenue at the end, then turn left. Continue past Cambridge Circus and cross the road, then continue to Greek Street, on your right. Walk up Greek Street to Soho Square Gardens, where you can rest for a few minutes and enjoy the small park and you might spot a few famous faces as the park is a well-known hangout for media and music personalities.

To the left side of the park as you enter it is Carlisle Street. Walk down Carlisle Street and you will find the pedestrianised Great Chapel Street. Turn right and walk to Sheraton Street which will be on your left. At the end of Sheraton Street is Wardour Street. Cross Wardour Street, turn right and immediately turn left into D'Arblay Street. At the end of D'Arblay Street you will find Poland Street, where you turn right and walk up to Great Marlborough Street on your left. If you walk to the end of Great Marlborough Street you will come to Regent Street, but don't go there just yet . . .

Nearby Attractions

If you walked to Great Marlborough Street you will have passed Seven Dials and Soho Square Gardens, as well as many famous streets in London's Soho district.

Great Marlborough Street was once a wealthy residential street, but it is now a commercial street, lined with shops, restaurants and a few other businesses. The main attraction of London's West End is shopping, so I hope you remembered your credit card.

Hamleys, the world-famous toy shop in Regent Street, is a wonderful experience, even if you don't have children, although you should avoid it at this point and save Hamleys until we visit Regent Street in the correct board order. The main shop you are likely to want to visit is Liberty's department store, which will be on your left just before Regent Street. Even if you don't go into Liberty's, remember to check out the clock, especially on the hour. Walking back along Great Marlborough Street from Liberty's you will find Carnaby Street, now on your right. You can walk the entire length of Carnaby Street, once famous for its smaller shops and stalls but these days more and more 'brands' are taking residence there. At the end of Carnaby Street, turn right into Beak Street, then left into Upper St John Street and you will find Golden Square, a formal open space with grass and gardens that was laid down in the 1670s by Sir Christopher Wren. Whilst in Golden Square you can look for the Stolperstein, a small brass plate in the pathway. It is, as far as I know, the only one in London and it commemorates Ada van Dantzig, who was arrested in France and murdered at Auschwitz on 14 February 1943 after she returned to the Netherlands, to rescue her family, who also became victims. After Golden Square the road becomes Lower St John Street. Follow it to Brewer Street and turn right. Bear right from Brewer Street into Glasshouse Street and at the end of Glasshouse Street is Regent Street.

This is where we encounter the "odd one out" on the Monopoly board, as it's not possible to get to our next destination, Vine Street, without trespassing into an adjoining property and we must briefly digress from strictly following the correct board order.

The Stolperstein commemorating Ada van Dantzig in Golden Square, Soho, London, prior to installation.

Stolpersteins are small brass plaques usually inserted into a path or pavement, but sometimes on a wall.
They are part of an ongoing Europe-wide project that was initiated by the German artist Gunter Demnig in 1992, which aims to commemorate individuals at exactly the last place of residency – or, sometimes, work – which was freely chosen by the person before they fell victim to Nazi terror.

Ada van Dantzig worked with Helmut Ruhemann, in his studio at number 2 Golden Square, before returning to The Netherlands in 1939 to try and help her family.

Former Vine Street police station (now closed)

Getting to Vine Street

It's impossible to get to Vine Street without going into another Monopoly property because it connects Regent Street to Piccadilly at each end and is actually situated in the Bond Street area of Mayfair, so it could count as visiting five properties at the same time, which will be useful information for those who simply want to visit all the properties as quickly as possible. So this is the one occasion where we are legitimately allowed to cheat and visit the Monopoly properties out of board order, although we'll keep our 'trespass' to a minimum.

At the end of Glasshouse Street, cross Regent Street and turn left, walking along Regent Street until you come to the wonderfully named, Man In Moon Passage. Walk down this passage and you will come to Vine Street.

Nearby Attractions

Vine Street always strikes me as being the odd one out on the Monopoly board, not just because of its location but because it is mostly just the backs of buildings that face onto Regent Street or Piccadilly, rather than somewhere you might choose to build a house or a hotel. Anyway, it's here so we must visit it, but you've probably seen most of the things worth seeing in the area by now, or you will see them at a later stage of the tour, so let's move on to our next property, which is Strand.

The Red Group

STRAND LONDON

FLEET STREET LONDON

TRAFALGAR SQUARE LONDON

Twinings Tea Shop on Strand.
Photo by Victorgrigas, shared under licence CC BY-SA 3.0

Getting to Strand

Now you could cheat again here, because if you walk to the end of Vine Street you will come to Piccadilly, however, if you want to do the properties as strictly in board order as possible, you'll need to stop short of Piccadilly, turn around and go back up Vine Street, through Man in Moon Passage again and back into Regent Street. When you emerge from Man in Moon Passage, turn right into Regent Street. Cross the road and continue along until you come to Shaftesbury Avenue on your left, cross over and you will find Piccadilly Circus Tube station. Take the Bakerloo Line on the Tube to Embankment Station.

When you leave Embankment station, walk through the Victoria Embankment Gardens (right next to the station). Watch out for Cleopatra's Needle, a 3,500-year-old Egyptian monolith situated on the Embankment next to the river. Continue through the gardens until you find the statue of Robert Raikes. On your left, there is an exit from the park into Savoy Place and opposite Carting Lane. Leave the park and walk up Carting Lane and you will come to Strand (usually called 'The' Strand by Londoners).

Nearby Attractions

As you walk up Carting Lane, keep an eye out on your left for the "Sewer Lamp", a unique street light which is fuelled by some of the gas being vented from London's sewers.

At Strand, turn left and a short way along on your left you will find the Art Deco Shell Mex House, which was built in 1931 and has the biggest clockface in the UK, with a diameter of 7.62 metres (25 feet). The faces of Big Ben are 6.9 metres (22.5 feet) in diameter. You may need to cross the road and peer through the trees to see the clock. Due to its location, even most Londoners are probably unaware of this clock, which, owing to its connection with the petrol industry, was nicknamed, "Big Benzine".

Turn around and retrace your steps to Carting Lane, then cross the road and you will be in front of the Coal Hole pub. This pub was formerly a coal store for the Savoy Hotel and its size gives some idea of just how much coal the hotel must have used before central heating was installed. Now it does a good lunch if you're feeling peckish.

Continuing past the pub you will come to the Savoy Hotel. Take note of the traffic, mostly London Black Cabs, as it enters and leaves the Savoy. This court is the only public access road in the UK where traffic drives on the right and not on the left. It is a privately owned road, so driving on the right does not contravene UK traffic regulations. The historical story is that in the horse and carriage days, ladies would traditionally sit behind the driver and it was easier for the groom or footman to open the carriage door for the ladies if the carriage was on the right side of the road.

Continue past the Savoy and you will reach Aldwych, where you should keep to your right and walk through the pedestrianised area. On your left you will see the church of St Mary Le Strand, an eighteenth-century church with great craftsmanship in evidence. If it's open, go inside and be sure to look up, as well as sideways.

When you've passed Aldwych you will see St Clement Danes, another, smaller, church that is well worth a visit. It was designed by Sir Christopher Wren and is now dedicated to the Royal Air Force. The inside is like a small museum of World War 2 flying.

Just past St Clement Danes, on the opposite side of the road, are the Royal Courts of Justice, built in the Gothic Revival style during the 1870s and opened in 1882. This is where the High Court and Court of Appeal are housed. It is one of the largest courts in Europe.

On your right, opposite the Law Courts, is Twinings Tea Shop. Do pop in and look around this 300-year-old shop - you won't regret it. There are hundreds of teas you can sample or buy and the staff are always welcoming and friendly and are only too pleased to share their knowledge with visitors.

Fleet Street, with St Pauls Cathedral in the distance.
Photo by Josep Renalias, shared under Licence CC BY-SA 3.0

Getting to Fleet Street

After you've visited Twinings (hopefully refreshed), turn right as you leave the shop and continue walking. As you pass the Temple Bar Memorial in the middle of the road, Strand becomes our next property, Fleet Street.

Nearby Attractions

You have seen, or will see on the way back, most of the nearby sights, however, there are a couple more churches that are worth seeing.

Opposite Chancery Lane is a small courtyard entrance beneath a Mock Tudor-style building. Walk under the building and along the path until you find Temple Church, an amazing building full of history that was originally constructed in the twelfth century by the Knights Templar. It is open most days until about four o'clock, but occasionally it closes earlier. When you've seen inside Temple Church, walk back to Fleet Street and turn right.

Fleet Street used to be the home of Britain's newspaper industry and there are still a few reminders to be seen as you walk, including the Art Deco clock outside what is now Peterborough Court. This clock was put in place during the 1920s rebuilding to replace an earlier clock. There are other interesting clocks to watch out for, too.

On your left, you will see Ye Old Cheshire Cheese, a historical pub that was rebuilt after the Great Fire of London in 1666 and was much visited by many literary characters, including Charles Dickens and Mark Twain.

Almost opposite Ye Old Cheshire Cheese is Whitefriars Street. Turn right into Whitefriars Street and a short way down on your right you will come to a footpath named Hanging Sword Alley. Due to redevelopment, the Alley doesn't look as you might expect it to, especially given its former name of Blood Bowl Alley, but it's one of the more unusually named paths you will find anywhere in London. If you walk through the alley you will come to Salisbury Square, which is on Salisbury Court, where you can see St Bride's church, another Wren church with a great history, that was rebuilt after the Great Fire of London. If you turn left into Salisbury Court, at the end you will be back in Fleet Street. Turn right and walk to Ludgate Circus.

At Ludgate Circus, look to your right and you will see Blackfriars Bridge, crossing the River Thames. Look straight across and you'll see St Paul's Cathedral. Turn to your left and you'll see the Old Bailey, the Central Criminal Court of England and Wales, where most of Britain's major criminal cases have been tried.

Also nearby and worth investigating if you have time are Postman's Park, Sir John Soane's Museum, Smithfield Market and Farringdon Station.

Trafalgar Square
Photo by David Iliff shared under license CC BY-SA 3.0

Getting to Trafalgar Square

From Ludgate Circus you can walk back along Fleet Street and Strand until you get to Charing Cross, or if you've had enough walking for a while, then hop on a number 11 or number 15 bus to save your legs. Cross the Strand at Charing Cross and you'll be in the southeast corner of Trafalgar Square.

Nearby Attractions

Almost next to you in the southeast corner is an ornamental light, which was built in 1926 as a replacement for a police box. It is commonly known as Britain's smallest police station and it could, theoretically, hold two prisoners, but it was actually built to house one policeman who observed the crowds to deter unruly behaviour. It is no longer needed by the police and is currently ignominiously used as a kind of broom cupboard by the Westminster City Council cleaning department.

Also in the Square itself, check out Nelson's Column, the Landseer Lions, the fountains and the four plinths, especially the fourth one, which has constantly changing contemporary art exhibits.

To the north of the Square is the National Gallery, which houses great works of art and is free to enter, although there is a charge for exhibitions in the National Portrait Gallery.

It's worth visiting St Martin in the Fields church, to the east. Be sure to go down to the coffee shop in the crypt and possibly do some brass rubbing.

Across the road from the Square, to the south, is a statue of King Charles 1st riding a horse and leading southwest away from the statue is the start of the Mall, which goes under Admiralty Arch and leads up to Buckingham Palace.

There is much within easy reach of Trafalgar Square that you may have seen earlier if you've followed this tour closely, but if you missed anything, now is a good opportunity to catch up before moving on to Fenchurch Street station.

Fenchurch Street Station and the Yellow Group

Fenchurch Street Station
Photograph by Hugh Llewelyn shared under licence CC BY-SA 2.0

Getting to Fenchurch Street Station

Walk back to Charing Cross, a little way along Strand and turn right into Villiers Street. Follow Villiers Street all the way down until you reach Embankment Tube station, then take the Circle or District Line to Tower Hill, giving your legs a well-earned rest for about twenty minutes. Leave Tower Hill station opposite the Tower of London and turn right into Trinity Square Gardens and find the Mercantile Marine Memorial, which commemorates merchant seamen lost during both World Wars. Leave the memorial and look at the church of All Hallows by the Tower on the opposite side of the road, then begin your five-minute walk to Fenchurch Street station by turning right along Byward Street until you reach Seething Lane, opposite All Hallows by the Tower, where you should turn right again. Walk along Seething Lane, past Pepys Street, until you reach the junction where the oddly named Crutched Friars heads right and Hart Street heads left. Turn left into Hart Street, then immediately right into New London Street. When you reach the end of New London Street, turn right into London Street and walk to Fenchurch Street Station.

Nearby Attractions

As well as the Tower of London and the other sights nearby you could visit the Gherkin, Lloyds of London Building, Leadenhall Market, the Bank of England and its museum and Mansion House, the official residence of the Lord Mayor of London, so we'll take a few of these in as we head toward our next property which is Leicester Square.

Leicester Square in 2012
Photo by Romazur, shared under licence CC BY-SA 3.0

Getting to Leicester Square

Leave Fenchurch Street Station and walk along Fenchurch Place until you reach Fenchurch Street, then turn left into Fenchurch Street and take the first right into Billiter Street. At the end of Billiter Street turn left into Leadenhall Street. Cross the road and turn right into St Mary Axe. At number 30 St Mary Axe is the Gherkin, a towering glass and steel structure, so named because of its shape. Turn left into Undershaft and pass St Mary's church, then take the pedestrian way on the right into Great St Helens. At the end of Great St Helens, turn left into Bishopsgate, go past Threadneedle Street and bear left, continuing along Bishopsgate until you come to a crossroads. At the crossroads, turn left into Leadenhall Street. A short way along Leadenhall Street on the right is the Lloyds Building, a modern building with all the infrastructure 'hung' on the outside, rather than concealed within. Just past the Lloyds Building, turn right into Lime Street to get a different view of the Lloyds Building, then turn right at the Philippine bank, into Leadenhall Place. At the end of Leadenhall Place you will find Leadenhall Market, a historic, Victorian, covered market with fine architecture, some nice shops and a couple of good pubs as well as some stalls. After exploring the small market, leave into Gracechurch Street and turn right. Walk to the crossroads and turn left into Cornhill. At the end of Cornhill you will arrive at Bank, where you will find the Mansion House, the Bank of England (visit the Bank of England museum if you have time) and the Royal Exchange.

You will also find Bank Tube station, where you can catch a Central Line train for three stops to Holborn then change to the Piccadilly Line and go two more stops to Leicester Square.

When you leave Leicester Square station, cross Charing Cross Road and walk along Cranbourn Street to arrive at Leicester Square.

Nearby Attractions

Most of the area around Leicester Square is designed to tempt you to spend money, with theatres, cinemas, casinos and shops everywhere.

Chinatown, a few minute's walk to the north of Leicester Square is a vibrant community with a distinct ambience and worth a walkthrough.

On the north side of the square you will find a statue of Harry Potter. Walk around the square and you will probably spot a few more famous statues, such as Paddington Bear, Bugs Bunny, Mary Poppins, Charlie Chaplin and even Shakespeare, among others. These statues are scattered, seemingly randomly, throughout the area.

On the west side is Swiss Court, flanked by M&M's World and the Lego Store. You can pop into M&M's World, which is interesting enough but to my mind is a glorified candy shop with prices to match, (so buy your M&Ms in a normal shop after you leave). Then have a walk around the Lego Store, which is the biggest Lego shop in Europe and is always interesting for children. Try to be there on the hour and see the Glockenspiel, in front of M&M's World, which plays music and has moving figures.

Café de Paris has been on Coventry Street since 1924
Photo by Andy Mabbett shared under licence CC BY-SA 3.0

Getting to Coventry Street

After you leave Swiss Court, cross over Whitcomb Street and you will be in Coventry Street.

Nearby Attractions

Most of the nearby interesting sights are covered in the Leicester Square and Piccadilly properties, as Coventry Street is quite a short street and although it has a little history of its own, it is, to all intents and purposes, absorbed into the general area of those other properties because Coventry Street directly connects Leicester Square and Piccadilly Circus at each of its ends. Nevertheless, there are a few attractive buildings that can be viewed, such as the Cafe de Paris.

Piccadilly in 1810, as seen from Hyde Park Corner

Getting to Piccadilly

At the end of Coventry Street you will be in Piccadilly Circus. Piccadilly Circus was once spectacularly surrounded by advertisements in neon lighting, however, probably due mostly to the high cost of renting advertising space, there is now only one building carrying illuminated advertisements and these are now illuminated by LED.

The main attraction is the Shaftesbury Memorial Fountain, topped by a statue of Anteros, the Greek God of requited love, although he is commonly mistaken for his brother, Eros, the God of love and sex. Continue across the pedestrianised area and cross Regent Street St James's and you will be at the start of Piccadilly.

Nearby Attractions

At just about a mile long and one of London's widest and straightest roads, Piccadilly is now one of London's foremost shopping streets, with stores such as Bentley & Skinner, Fortnum & Mason and Hatchards, which claims to be the oldest bookshop in the United Kingdom. There is also a wonderful example of an early shopping mall at Burlington Arcade. If you visit Burlington Arcade, be sure to take a look at Hancocks. The Victoria Cross is Britain's highest award for gallantry in the presence of the enemy and Hancocks is the jeweller that makes all of the Victoria Cross medals awarded and has done so since the medal's inception in 1856. Remember to keep your credit cards firmly in your pocket, these are not cheap souvenir shops.

Take a short diversion up Berkeley Street to Berkeley Square and you may hear a nightingale singing, if you can believe Frank Sinatra and Bing Crosby. In any case, it's a pleasant place to sit and rest your legs for a while.

At the end of Piccadilly you will come to the Ritz hotel on your left, next to Green Park. Walk down the pathway alongside the Ritz and you will come to Spencer House, built by the ancestral family of

Princess Diana. The building is only open on Sundays and there is an entrance fee, but even if you don't go in, it's nice to see the outside.
Continue along the path to Lancaster House, then head right, to see the Canada Memorial to the fallen Canadians of both World Wars. There is also a reasonable coffee shop near the memorial garden.
Outside the gate you will see the Victoria Memorial, Constitution Hill and Buckingham Palace.
Walk up Constitution Hill to the Wellington Arch. To your right, just back into Piccadilly, is the Bomber Command war memorial. You will also see the New Zealand War Memorial in the centre of the grassy island where Wellington Arch is.

Postcard image by J Arthur Dixon Shared under licence CC by SA 2.0

The Green Group

REGENT STREET
LONDON

OXFORD STREET
LONDON

BOND STREET
LONDON

The Apple Store on Regent Street
Photo by Tony Webster shared under licence CC BY-SA 3.0

Getting to Regent Street

If you don't mind walking fifteen minutes or so back along Piccadilly, then go back to Piccadilly Circus. Alternatively, you can walk around the Wellington Arch, keeping it on your right and avoiding Park Lane, which we will return to when we visit the blue group and find Hyde Park Corner Tube station, then take the Piccadilly Line Tube for a few minutes ride to Piccadilly Circus.

When you leave Piccadilly Circus station, Regent Street is in front of you and to your right.

Nearby Attractions

The sights worth seeing in and around Regent Street have been mentioned earlier in the Marlborough Street and Piccadilly properties and you've been here before when you were allowed the 'legal cheat' to see Vine Street, so don't spend too much time here, except for visiting Hamley's.

Cross the road and walk up Regent Street until you get to Oxford Circus.

Oxford Street
Photo from Oast House Archive shared under licence CC BY-SA 2.0

Getting to Oxford Street

Oxford Street crosses Regent Street and runs right as far as Tottenham Court Road and left as far as Marble Arch.

Nearby Attractions

Oxford Street is probably London's premier shopping street, with just about every major chain store featuring somewhere, but other than the shopping experience, there's not too much to interest most tourists.

I would recommend turning left, toward Marble Arch. On the north side of the road is Twist Museum, which is packed with illusions and good fun, if your budget stretches to almost £20 each for entrance. If not, continue on the south side and you will come to New Bond Street on your left.

The Allies. Franklin D Roosevelt and Winston Churchill
Photo by Anthony O'Neil shared under licence CC BY-SA 2.0

Getting to Bond Street

Bond Street, much like Marlborough Street, does not actually exist but is two streets joined together and the name is more of a concept than an actual street. The concept is that of a high-end shopping precinct and the two roads are New Bond Street and Old Bond Street.

Nearby Attractions

It is an urban myth that the area has any connection with the famous fictional spy, 007 James Bond. The street was originally made across some fields by Sir Thomas Bond in the 1600s and was developed further during the 1720s after it became established as a fashionable place for the wealthy to meet and socialise. Sir Thomas Bond was a kind of accountant for Queen Henrietta Maria, who was the wife of King Charles 1st. The street is named after Sir Thomas and the distinction between New and Old isn't widely used in everyday matters.

The area known as Bond Street is home to many upmarket fashion retailers and to other prestigious businesses, including the auction houses of Bonham's and Sotheby's and the Jeweller Tiffany's.

It will take you about half an hour to walk the entire length of Bond Street to Piccadilly and back again and is worth the walk if you want to see some older and smaller shopfronts. Redevelopment is quite tightly controlled in the area to try and preserve much of its character.

There is a sculpture called "The Allies" of Winston Churchill and Franklin D. Roosevelt sitting on a bench and there is just enough space between them for you to sit and grab a unique photo opportunity.

When you get back to Oxford Street you should turn left and after a minute's walk you will come to Bond Street Tube station. Resist the temptation to walk down to Marble Arch, as we will get there when we visit Park Lane, but first, we have to go back to the east end of London to visit Liverpool Street Station.

Liverpool Street Station

Inside Liverpool Street Station
Photo by Irid Escent shared under licence CC BY-SA 2.0

Getting to Liverpool Street Station

Go into Bond Street Tube station and catch a Central Line train all the way to Liverpool Street, which will take between ten and fifteen minutes. There are exits from the Tube both inside and outside the main railway station, so be sure to go into the main Liverpool Street Station. When you leave, exit onto Bishopsgate.

Nearby Attractions

You will already have seen some of the nearby sights to the west of Liverpool Street when you walked from Fenchurch Street Station to Bank, but there are some gems on the northern and eastern sides, too.

As you leave Liverpool Street station onto Bishopsgate, cross the road and turn left. You will see Dirty Dick's pub, which is over 200 years old and has a galleried interior. Pop in (you can get coffee as well as beer) and ask the staff to tell you the story behind the name.

After you pass (or leave) Dirty Dick's, continue eastward to your right and the first street is Middlesex Street, the site of the famous Petticoat Lane Market. If you happen to be here on a Sunday there will be a vibrant market, possibly London's busiest, on Middlesex Street and the surrounding streets. Take your map, as it might become confusing wandering from street to street and you'll need to get back to Bishopsgate when you're finished.

Continuing along Bishopsgate, the road name changes and becomes Norton Folgate and on your right will be Folgate Street. A short way down Folgate Street is Dennis Severs House, a Georgian building that has been preserved by its former owner, Dennis Severs, in the manner in which it would have been when it was occupied by Huguenot silk weavers around 1700. It's not a cheap visit and totally unsuitable for those with mobility difficulties, as it has steep stairs and is dimly lit, but if it is an era of history that interests you it is worth half an hour or so of your time.

Between Folgate Street and Middlesex Street you will also find Spitalfields Market, which began as a fruit and vegetable market in 1682 with a charter from King Charles 2nd, although it is much changed these days.

When you leave Dennis Severs House continue down Folgate Street and turn left into Elder Street. Continue walking and you will cross Fleur De Lis Street, then cross the main road, Commercial Street, and walk into Quaker Street. Follow Quaker Street as it bends right, then turn left into Braithwaite Street. These, and other, street names all recollect the days when the area was occupied by Huguenot and Quaker refugees. Braithwaite Street becomes a footpath and emerges next to Shoreditch High Street Station, onto Bethnal Green Road. You are now in London's East End, once a hive of villainy and a den of inequity, but these days it is one of the most trendy place places in London.

On your left in Bethnal Green Road is the Boxpark shopping arcade, which is made from old steel shipping containers and although quite small in size it is worth a quick look as it is said to be the first of its type in the world.

A few minutes walk along Bethnal Green Road to your right will bring you to Brick Lane. Turn right into Brick Lane and you will find London's two famous beigel shops, which are open 24 hours every day. Treat yourself to a salt-beef beigel. I've eaten them in lots of places and these really are the best I've ever had. One shop is older than the other, but the quality is equally good in both, so choose the one with the shortest queue. If you want to explore further along Brick Lane you'll find the busiest and most commercial part of the market area.

The whole area around you was once fields but over the centuries became built up due to waves of immigrants and refugees into London. In the 17th century, there were French Huguenots, then the Irish came, followed by Ashkenazi Jews escaping from Europe and the pogroms in Russia. Today the area is home to many Bengalis and you'll notice the street names are written in Bangladeshi as well as in English.

Indeed, the reason there are so many Sunday markets in the area is that the British government in the 19th century gave special dispensation to the Jewish community, as there were no markets open on the Christian sabbath, and the orthodox Jews couldn't attend the Saturday, Jewish sabbath, markets. Many of the non-market places in the area these days take advantage of the visitor trade to the markets by opening on Sundays but are closed on Mondays, so choose your day to visit accordingly.

Retrace your steps back along Bethnal Green Road, cross over and on the right is Chance Street (you could count that as an 'extra' place on the Monopoly board if you want to). Walk down Chance Street, cross over Old Nichol Street and continue down Camlet Street. You will find Arnold Circus, a circular road with a small park, Boundary Gardens, in the centre. This is the Boundary Estate and is where London made its first recorded attempt to clean up the slums and improve the lives of the poor people in the area, then called 'The Old Nichol', which was so overcrowded and insanitary that more than a quarter of all babies died before they reached their first birthday. It was also, arguably, the first attempt of its kind in the world where civic authorities tried to create decent social housing conditions. The history of London's poor and the story of the rookeries they lived in deserves a whole book of its own and others have chronicled the tale far better than I can, so if you're a fan of social history and you want to know more, look it up and enjoy, it's a fascinating subject. Meanwhile, back to the tour.

The street adjacent to Camlet Street is Club Row, which was once home to a busy animal market, where East Londoners would trade pets such as cats, dogs and birds. Back in the 1960s there was more than one story of a customer buying what they were told was a canary, only to get home and find the dye slowly came off to reveal a common sparrow.

If you leave Arnold Circus on the opposite side, via Hocker Street, you will come to Virginia Road. Turn right and bear left as you pass the small park called Virginia Gardens, then turn right into Columbia Road. After a couple of minutes you will find the Flower Market, open on Sundays and one of London's brightest and most colourful markets and hands down the best flower market in the whole of London.

If you continue through the market and along to the end of Columbia Road you will come to Hackney Road. There are a few museums in the area and two are especially worth visiting, but unfortunately are in opposite directions. However, there is a pleasant and surprising bonus in store for those who choose to visit both . . .

Cross Hackney Road and turn left, walk up to Cremer Street and turn right then walk to the end, where you will find Kingsland Road. Turn right onto Kingsland Road and you'll come to Geffrye Museum, now called the Museum of the Home. This museum is housed in a group of old almshouses and has rooms decorated and furnished to display how homes have changed over the last four hundred years.

After visiting the Museum of the Home, retrace your steps back to Hackney Road and as you leave Cremer Street, turn left. After another five minutes or so you will come to a park on your left. Immediately after the park, turn left into Goldsmith's Row. A short way down is a pleasant surprise - who would expect to find a farmyard in the middle of London? Hackney City Farmyard has sheep, chickens, goats, geese and horses, among other animals and is free to visit. It's a great place to take a short break for 45 minutes or so, especially if you have children and there is an Italian cafe, too, which serves very good coffee.

When you leave the farmyard, go back to Hackney Road and turn left, walk about ten minutes to the end, then turn right and cross Cambridge Heath Road, after a few minutes, on your left you will discover the Museum of Childhood, with a fascinating collection of children's games, toys and related activities through the centuries and entrance is free.

There is so much more to this part of London than most people realise, and you could easily spend a few days exploring if you have the time, but for now we have to leave, as it's time to head back to the West End and visit our penultimate property, Park Lane.

The Dark Blue Group

Park Lane, showing Hyde Park on the left
Photo by Mike Smith shared under licence CC BY-SA 2.0

Getting to Park Lane

After you visit the Museum of Childhood you can catch a Central Line Tube train from Bethnal Green station right outside and rest your legs all the way to Marble Arch. The main road opposite the station is Park Lane, but don't go there just yet . . .

Nearby Attractions

Leave Marble Arch Station and in front of you is Marble Arch. The Arch was designed by Robert Nash and was once an entrance to Buckingham Palace. It was moved to its present location when Queen Victoria had the Palace enlarged to accommodate her growing family. There is an urban myth that it was moved because it isn't wide enough for the State Coach to pass through, but this is untrue and in fact the State Coach passed under the Arch during Queen Elizabeth 2nd's coronation procession in 1953.

Turn right as you leave Marble Arch station and walk along Bayswater Road to the major road on your right, which is Edgware Road. You will need to cross Edgware Road in two phases, utilising the island in the middle. This island is the site of the Tyburn Tree, which, despite its name, was never actually a tree. It was the wooden gallows where many of London's most notorious criminals were publicly hanged. The last public execution at Tyburn was that of highway robber John Austin, on 3rd November 1783.

Leave the island via the pedestrian crossing which takes you onto the other side of Bayswater Road and the Marble Arch Fountains. From there you can walk up to Marble Arch and get a closer look at the structure.

Head south, toward Hyde Park and cross Cumberland Gate, keeping right as you go. Continue walking south along the path in the park and you will reach Speaker's Corner, where it's said that anyone can set up their soapbox and preach their opinion on just about anything to the crowds. In reality, free speech is allowed anywhere in Britain as long as it's lawful and Speakers Corner is no exception, so if you are going to make a speech, make sure you adhere to the law or you may find yourself being arrested.

A little further on you should take the path on your right, which leads to Brook Gate and you can cross the road to see the Animals in War Memorial.

You are now in the middle of Park Lane.

Burlington Arcade in Mayfair
Photo by Andrew Dunn shared under licence CC BY-SA 2.5

Getting to Mayfair

Continue across Park Lane and walk into Upper Brook Street, by the Aston Martin showroom.
You are now in Mayfair.

Nearby Attractions

Mayfair isn't a street, but much like the concept area of Bond Street, it is an area comprising many streets and squares, including Grosvenor Square, the former home of the American Embassy (until 2017), which you will reach if you continue walking along Upper Brook Street. It is, however, an area which is more clearly defined and it includes the Bond Street concept area, with its boundaries commonly recognised as being Park Lane to the west, Piccadilly to the south, Regent Street to the east and Oxford Street to the north.
Just as in the game, Mayfair is the most expensive area to buy property in London, with average house prices in 2023 reaching upwards of £3,500,000.

The End

And there you have it - congratulations on successfully visiting all the Monopoly properties in the order in which they appear on the Monopoly board (except for the impossible exception at Vine Street, of course).
You can leave Grosvenor Square and walk up North Audley Street to Oxford Street and stop at the Mayfair Chippy on the way to treat yourself to cod & chips, a favourite British food, before you make your weary way back to your hotel for a well-earned rest.

Alternatives

Of course, visiting each Monopoly property in the order it appears on the board is time-consuming, due to doubling back on yourself and taking circuitous routes to avoid other visiting other properties out of sequence. Most visitors to London will want to make the most of their available time and there are several ways in which you might choose to do this, depending on your personal interest and time constraints.

Here is one suggested way to use the Monopoly tour in 'bite-sized chunks'. Read the guide, of course, and do some additional research to discover other nearby places that interest you, then choose one of the groups listed below.

You will probably need to consult your map for most of these suggestions, as parts of the walks are from directions that differ from the book.

If you're really strapped for time and can't or don't want to do the whole tour but still want to see some of London that most tourists miss, then my recommendation is to prioritise the walks around Liverpool Street Station and the Red Group.

Brown Group and Fenchurch Street Station
There really isn't much in Old Kent Road to interest most visitors, so if time is tight, just don't go there. Instead, start at Whitechapel Station and do the walk in reverse as far as Tower Hill, then walk to Fenchurch Street Station. Allow about two hours for this walk.

It's a ten-minute walk from Fenchurch Street Station to Liverpool Street Station, but you can take a little longer and see the Bank of England, Leadenhall Market etc as described on page 71.

Liverpool Street Station
This is worthy of a walk on its own. Allow at least half a day for this walk.

Light Blue Group and Kings Cross Station
Start at Angel Islington and walk to Kings Cross Station via Pentonville Road and Euston Road. Allow about two hours for this walk.

Pink Group
Combine this with the Yellow Group. Start at Hyde Park Corner and walk along Piccadilly and Coventry Street to Leicester Square, then turn right and head south toward Trafalgar Square and cross Strand into Northumberland Avenue. Walk almost to the bottom of Northumberland Avenue then turn right into Whitehall Place and walk to Whitehall. Allow about three hours for this walk.

Orange Group
Bow Street and Marlborough Street make a decent short walk, but there's really nothing to see in Vine Street and if you really want to see it it's probably a better use of time to include it in the Yellow Group, as it is off Piccadilly, or the Green Group, off Regent Street.

Indeed, I would be tempted to combine the Orange and Green Groups into a single walk, which should probably take around three hours.

Red Group
I think the Red Group makes an interesting walk, but I would start at St Pauls Tube station, take in St Pauls Cathedral and walk down to Ludgate Circus, then along Fleet Street, continue along Strand and arrive at Trafalgar Square. This is approximately a two-and-a-half-hour walk.

Yellow Group
The Yellow Group can easily include elements from the Pink Group, as above.

Green Group
I would combine the Green Group with the Orange Group, as above.

Dark Blue Group and Marylebone Station
I would start this at Marylebone Station, visit the Sherlock Holmes Museum if it interests you and take a walk in Regents Park, then head south, cross Marylebone Road and walk along until you find Robert Adam Street on your left, then visit The Wallace Collection.

After the Wallace Collection, continue south to Oxford Street, turn right to Marble Arch and pick up the Dark Blue Group from there. Allow about two hours for this walk.

Printed in Great Britain
by Amazon